Fine Line in association with Rough Fiction and
Park Theatre present the World Premiere of

DISTANCE

By Alex McSweeney

Published by Playdead Press 2018

© Alex McSweeney 2018

Alex McSweeney has asserted his rights under the Copyright, Design and Patents Act, 1988, to be identified as the author of this work.

A CIP catalogue record for this book is available from the British Library.

ISBN 978-1-910067-68-0

Caution

All rights whatsoever in this play are strictly reserved and application for performance should be sought through the author before rehearsals begin. No performance may be given unless a license has been obtained.

This book is sold subject to the condition that it shall not by way of trade or otherwise, be lent, resold, hired out, or otherwise circulated without the publisher's prior consent in any form of binding or cover other than that in which it is published and without a similar condition including this condition being imposed on the subsequent purchaser.

Playdead Press
www.playdeadpress.com

DISTANCE was first performed at Park Theatre on 5 September 2018 with the following cast and creative team:

CAST
Doreene Blackstock | Folami/Ticket Inspector/Waitress
Adam Burton | Steven
Richard Corgan | The Duke
Lindsay Fraser | Sonja
Abdul Salis | Alan

CREATIVES
Alex McSweeney | Writer
Simon Pittman | Director
Bethany Wells | Designer
Dan Saggars | Lighting Designer
Alexandra Faye Braithwaite | Sound Designer
Ian William Galloway | Video Designer
Fine Line | Producer
Rough Fiction | Associate Producer
Celia Dugua | General Manager
Jane Arnold-Forster | Production Manager
Kate Eccles | Stage Manager
Julie Holman & Nick Pearce for Target Live | Public Relations
Mobius Industries | Print Distribution
Mann Bros | Video Production
Graham Turner | Art Work

With thanks to:
Arts Council England, CALM, Joseph Croft, John Chambers, Lynette Charles and Deborah King from Mind Haringey, Ann Devine, English Touring Theatre, John Fairbairn, Alison and John Fraser, Hannah Kalmanowitz from the Stuart Low Trust, Gill Foster, the theatre tech team and everyone at London South Bank University, Melli Marie, Mesmer, Andrew Nasrat, Vicky Richardson, Chris Riddlestone, Park Theatre, The Royal Victoria Hall Foundation, Stage One, Fana Sunley-Smith, and Henrietta Webb-Wilson.

Special thanks to the actors who helped developed *Distance*:
Anthony Barclay, Madeleine Bowyer, John Cummins, Michelle Greenidge, Richard James-Neale, Debbie Korley, Christopher Lane, Richard Mylan, Mark Parsons, Ben Mars, Simon Scardifield, Daniel Taylor, Yasmin Gava, Kingsley Mpofu and Edmund Wiseman.

Distance was first developed on Park Theatre's Script Accelerator Programme 2016 and is kindly supported by Arts Council England, The Royal Victoria Hall Foundation and Stage One.

Doreene Blackstock | Folami/Ticket Inspector/Waitress

Theatre includes: *Much Ado About Nothing* (The Globe), *Roundelay* (Southwark Playhouse), *Cymbeline, Hamlet, Noughts & Crosses* (RSC), *Antigone, Loneliness of the Long Distance Runner* (Pilot Theatre Company), *Holloway Jones* (Synergy Theatre Project), *The Container* (Young Vic Theatre), *Any Which Way* (Only Connect Theatre), *One Under, The Gift* (Tricycle Theatre), *25/7* (Talking Birds Theatre Company), *Document Given To Me By a Young Lady from Rwanda* (Ice & Fire Theatre Company), *The Carver Chair* (Contact Theatre), *Leave Taking, Girlie Talk* (Belgrade Studio), *Rosie & Jim's Big Adventure* (Ragdoll Theatre Company), *Leonora's Dance* (Black Theatre Co-operative).

TV and Film includes: *Sex Education* (Netflix), *Death in Paradise, The Child in Time, EastEnders, The Game, Silent Witness, Trinity, The Bill, Life Begins, Family Business, Wire in the Blood, Medics, Casualty, Holby City, Judge John Deed, Gimme Gimme Gimme, Tom Jones, Common as Muck, Mm Hm, This Year's Love*.

Adam Burton | Steven

Trained at LIPA.

Theatre includes: *Jerusalem, All My Sons* (Watermill Theatre), *My Brilliant Friend* (Rose Theatre), *The Tempest* (Norwich & Norfolk Festival), *Calculating Kindness* (Undercurrent Theatre), *The Hairy Ape, The Dutchess Of Malfi* (Old Vic), *Everyman* (National Theatre), *Titus* (The Theory of Everything), *The Drowned Man, Masque of the Red Death*, and *Faust* (Punchdrunk), *You*

Can't Take It With You (Manchester Royal Exchange), *The Orphan Of Zhao, Boris Godunov, A Life of Galileo, American Trade, King Lear, Anthony and Cleopatra, The Winter's Tale, The Drunk,* and *Julius Caesar* (RSC), *The Tempest* (RSC in a Suitcase), *Timon of Athens* and *A Midsummer Nights Dream* (The Globe), *As You Like It* (Derby Playhouse), *Baggage* (Edinburgh Pleasance Theatre), *The Adding Machine, Heat of a Dog* (Rogue State), *The Waiting Game* (Courtyard, King's Head).

Television includes: *Bloody Queens: Elizabeth and Mary* (Pioneer Productions), *RMS Titanic: Case Closed* (Bedlam), *Doctors* (BBC), *Jekyll* (Hartswood Films), *Casualty* (BBC), *Happy on the Boat* (Hewland), *Dangerfield* (BBC), *Treflan* (S4C).

Film includes: *Alice Though the Looking Glass* (Absolem Productions), *The Butcher's Shop* (Haas Films – Open Award-Venice Film Festival), Short/Film (Carioca – Best short nominee Austin Film Festival), Breaker (Winners Productions – Finalist NPA Shorts; Golden Lion Film Festival), Brown Paper Bag (Dreamfinder – BAFTA best short).

Richard Corgan | The Duke

Trained at Bristol Old Vic Theatre School.

Theatre includes: *The Pulverised* (Arcola Theatre), *Growth (Fringe 1st Award), Love Lies & Taxidermy, I got Superpowers for my Birthday* (Paines Plough), *Tom: A Story of Tom Jones The Musical* (UK. Tour), *NSFW* (Waking Exploits), *Merchant of Venice* (Singapore Repertory Theatre), *Gardening: For the Unfulfilled and Alienated (Fringe 1st Award)* (Undeb Theatre), *A Provincial Life* (National Theatre Wales), *Taming Of The Shrew, Macbeth, Twelfth Night* (Ripley Castle), *Flowers From Tunisia* (Torch Theatre),

Taming of the Shrew (The Globe), *Frozen, Merlin and the Cave of Dreams* (Sherman Cymru), *It's About Me* (Hampstead Theatre), *Money & Science & Me* (Liverpool Everyman), *The Long, The Short & The Tall* (Pleasance, Islington), *Macbeth, The Changeling* (Barbican Theatre).

TV includes: Series regular in *Baker Boys* for 2 Series (BBC), *Doctors (BBC)*, *Casualty (BBC)*, *Caught in the Web (BBC)*, *The B World* (BBC), *Pobol Y Cwm* (S4C).

Film includes: *A Fistful of Lead* (Nightshooter Films), *Loki's Game* (Trickster Films) *The Red Haven* (Tornado Studios), *Nightshooters* (Nightshooter Films), *Canaries* (Maple Dragon), *Diana* (Ecosse Films), *Magpie* (Nowhere Fast Productions), *Colin* (Nowhere Fast Productions), *Hindsight* (Ignition Films).

Radio includes: *Foursome* (BBC Radio 4), *Blue Remembered Hills* (Christchurch Studios), *Great Ormond St Charity Concert St Paul's* (LBC).

Lindsay Fraser | Sonja
Trained at East 15 Acting School.

For Park Theatre: *Out of the Cage*

Theatre includes: *Execution Of Justice* (Southwark Playhouse), *Just So Stories* (The Kings Head), and *Oh Go My Man* (Tristan Bates Theatre).

Film includes: *Touch* (Largo Films), *Still Waters* (Memoir Pictures), In Control, and *The Passenger* (Thirty-Two Films), *Jacob* (Pigtail Productions), *Cygnus* (I Am The Sand Man), *Judith, Collateral Damage* (NFTS), and *Hard Light* (Major Arcana / LFS).

Abdul Salis | Alan

Theatre credits include: *The Barbershop Chronicles* (National Theatre), *Birth!* (Manchester Royal Exchange), *War Horse* (National Theatre), *Boy* (Almeida), *The Rise and Shine of Comrade Fiasco* (The Gate), *Lungs*, *The Initiate* and *The Human Ear* (Paines Plough), *Joe Guy* (Tiata Fahodzi at Soho Theatre), *Don Juan in Soho* (Donmar Warehouse) and most recently *31 Hours* (The Bunker Theatre).

TV includes: *Father Brown* (BBC), *Urban Myths 'Public Enemy'* (Happy Tramp), *Power Monkeys* (Hat Trick), *Doctors* (Blunt Pictures), *Hacks* (Hat Trick), *Strike Back* (Leftbank Pictures), *Outnumbered* (Hat Trick), *Victoria Wood Christmas Special* (Phil McIntyre Productions), *Casualty* (BBC), *Doctor Who* (Kudos), *Gifted* (Red Productions), *Trevor's World of Sport* (Hat Trick), *Roger Roger* (BBC) and *The Hidden City* (Hallmark).

Film includes: *Trendy* (A 6 Foot Barrel), *Flyboys* (Electric), *Welcome Home* (Wega-Film) and *Love Actually* (Working Title).

Alex McSweeney | Writer

Alex is an actor, playwright and director. His writing / directing credits include: *Out Of The Cage* (Park Theatre), *A Hero Of Our Time* (Rose Theatre Kingston and Zoo Edinburgh), and *Between Women* (Hen and Chickens).

His new play / collaboration, *Crossing Borders / Fragments* with Velina Hasu Houston premiered in June 2018 (Martin Massman Theatre, Los Angeles & Ryerson Theatre, Toronto)

As an actor he has worked extensively across television, film, theatre and radio. Most recently, he appeared in *Nyela's Dream*, *Endeavour* and *Call The Midwife*, as well as regular collaborations with Steven Berkoff including *On The*

Waterfront (Nottingham Playhouse and Theatre Royal Haymarket) and *Oedipus* (Liverpool Playhouse).

Alex developed *Distance* on Park Theatre's Script Accelerator in 2016.

Simon Pittman | Director

Simon is a theatre director and movement director. He co-directs the theatre company Rough Fiction and is Associate Director (Learn & Train) at Frantic Assembly. Simon trained on the Birkbeck Theatre Directing MFA, the NT Studio Director's Course, and as movement associate to Steven Hoggett and Scott Graham. He was resident director at The Library Theatre Manchester 2006 / 07.

Direction includes: *The Expected* (Wilton's Music Hall), *Othello* (The Ambassadors, West End with National Youth Theatre & Frantic Assembly), *Not A Game for Boys* (Library Theatre Manchester), *His Wild Imaginings* (LSO St Luke's), *The Last of The Lake* (Brighton Dome & Tour). As Associate: *The Go Between* (West Yorkshire Playhouse), *Floyd Collins* (Southwark Playhouse), *The Shawshank Redemption* (Edinburgh Festival / Gaiety Theatre).

Movement direction includes: *The Comedy of Errors* (Royal Shakespeare Company), *The Box of Delights* (Wilton's Music Hall), *The Rivals* (Watermill Theatre), *Out of The Cage* (Park Theatre), *The Kingdom* (Soho Theatre), *The White Bike* (The Space), *The Shawshank Redemption* (Edinburgh Festival / Gaiety Theatre), *Between Two Worlds* (Sherman Theatre), *Mixter Maxter, 99…100* (National Theatre of Scotland). As Associate: *The Go-Between* (Apollo Theatre, West End), *The Curious Incident of The Dog In The* Night-time (Gielgud Theatre, West End), *365* (EIF / National Theatre of Scotland).

Bethany Wells | Designer

Trained in architecture, Bethany is a performance designer working across dance, theatre and installation, with a particular interest in site-specific and devised performance. Bethany is an Associate Artist with Middle Child Theatre, Hull.

Recent work includes: *Legacy* (York Theatre Royal), *TRUST* (Gate Theatre), *Party Skills for the End of the World (*Nigel Barrett and Louise Mari), *The Department of Distractions* (Third Angel), *All We Ever Wanted Was Everything* (Middle Child), *Cosmic Scallies* (Graeae & Royal Exchange), *We Were Told There Was Dancing* (Royal Exchange Young Company), *Removal Men* (Yard Theatre), *Dark Corners* (Polar Bear), *Seen and Not Heard* (Complicite Creative Learning), *The Desire Paths* (Third Angel), *The Factory* (Royal Exchange Young Company), *THE FUTURE* (Company 3), *Late Night Love* (Eggs Collective), *Live Art Dining* (Live Art Bistro), *Race Cards*, (Selina Thompson), *Correspondence* (Old Red Lion), *Partus* (Third Angel), *My Eyes Went Dark* (Finborough Theatre), *WINK* (Theatre 503).

Bethany is currently working on, *WARMTH*, a wood-fired mobile sauna and performance space, commissioned by Compass Live Art and touring nationally.

Dan Saggars | Lighting Designer

Design credits include: *The Expected* (Wilton's Music Hall), *Schism* (Park Theatre), *Eugene Onegin* (Mid Wales Opera), *How To Win Against History* Tour 2017 (Young Vic, Seiriol Davies and Aine Flanagan Productions), *Chocolate Cake* and *The Borrowers* (Polka Theatre) *Orfeo et Euridice* and *Alcina* (Longborough Festival Opera), *Sherlock Holmes and the Crimson Cobbles* (The Theatre, Chipping Norton), *Dad Dancing* (Second Hand Dance and Battersea Arts Centre), *Tidy Up* (Peut-Être Theatre), *Punts* (Theatre503), *Carry On Jaywick* (Vaults Festival and touring), *Laura Lindow's Then Leap!* (The Lowry, Manchester and rural touring), *Echo_Narcissus* (The Yard Theatre).

Alexandra Faye Braithwaite | Sound Designer
For Park Theatre: *Happy to Help*.

Theatre includes: *Talking Heads* (West Yorkshire Playhouse), *Toast* (The Lowry & Traverse Edinburgh), *GROTTY* (The Bunker), *Acceptance* (Hampstead Downstairs), *Grumpy Old Women III* (UK Tour), *Chicken Soup* (Sheffield Crucible Studio), *Dublin Carol* (The Sherman), *Kanye the First* (Hightide Festival), *Room* (Theatre Royal Stratford East / National Theatre of Ireland), *If I Was Queen* (Almeida), *Rudolph* (West Yorkshire Playhouse), *The Remains of Maisie Duggan* (National Theatre of Ireland), *Torch* (New Diorama), *The Tempest* (Royal & Derngate), *Simon Slack* (Soho), *Diary of a Madman* (The Gate & Traverse, Edinburgh), *The Rolling Stone* (Orange Tree – Nominated For Off West End Award For "Best Sound Design"), *The Future* (The Yard), *My Beautiful Black Dog* (Southbank Centre), *Hamlet Is Dead, No Gravity* (Arcola), *Juicy & Delicious* (Nuffield Theatre), *Remote* (Theatre Royal Plymouth), *The Shelter* (Riverside Studios) and *Lonely Soldiers* (Arts Theatre).

Ian William Galloway | Video Designer
Theatre work includes: *Mosquitoes* (National Theatre), *Singin' in The Rain, Gypsy, Elf: The Musical* (West End), *What Is The City But The People?* (MIF), *Schikaneder* (Raimund Theatre, Vienna), *Wendy & Peter Pan* (Royal Shakespeare Company), *The Absence of War, Spring Awakening, A Midsummer Night's Dream* (Headlong), *Dry Powder, Prism, Hapgood* (Hampstead Theatre), *Oh What A Lovely War* (Theatre Royal Stratford East), *Beautiful Burnout, Lovesong* (Frantic Assembly), *Macbeth, The Missing* (National Theatre of Scotland), *Amadeus* (Chichester Festival Theatre), *The Graduate, Enjoy* (West Yorkshire Playhouse), *The Radicalisation of Bradley Manning, Mother Courage and her Children* (National Theatre Wales), *Est-ce Que Tu Dors?* (Festival d'Avignon / Complicite), *The Tempest, The Lion In Winter* (Theatre Royal Haymarket).

Opera work includes: *La Fanciulla Del West* (La Scala), *Madame Butterfly* (Glyndebourne), *Hansel & Gretel* (Opera North), *Agrippina* (Theatre an der Wien), *The Marriage of Figaro* (English National Opera), *Eugene Onegin* (ENO & Metropolitan Opera), *Faust* (Mariinsky Theatre), *The Flying Dutchman* (Scottish Opera), *Juliette, Where the Wild Things Are* (Bremer Oper), *The Lion's Face, Seven Angels* (The Opera Group), *Hotel de Pekin* (Nationale Reisopera), *Sancta Susanna, Von Heute Auf Morgen* (Opera de Lyon).

Fine Line | Producer

Fine Line was founded in 2011 and predominately works with new writing. We produce theatre that challenges and excites our audience, with most of our work having a strong political and social message at its heart.

Fine Line's credits include: *Moormaid* (Arcola Theatre), *Out Of The Cage* (Park Theatre), *Even Stillness Breathes Softly Against A Brick Wall* (Soho Theatre). *When Did You Last See My Mother?* (Trafalgar Studios), *Execution Of Justice* (Southwark Playhouse). Fine Line is a recipient of the Stage One New Producers Bursary for 2014, 2015 and 2017, and is currently supported by English Touring Theatre talent development programme ETT Forge.

Rough Fiction | Associate Producer

Founded by Simon Pittman and Phil Tattersall-King, Rough Fiction is a UK theatre company making work through cross-arts collaboration, working with a range of artists and co-producers. The company creates original productions that explore contemporary culture, with a focus on interdisciplinary collaboration and storytelling.

Productions include: *The Expected* (Wilton's Music Hall), *His Wild Imaginings* (LSO St Luke's), *The Last of The Lake* (Brighton Dome and Tour), *Killing Alan* (Underbelly Edinburgh), *Hospitals and Other Buildings That Catch Fire* (Underbelly & NSDF).

The company also ran an Ensemble Laboratory between 2010 and 2014 first hosted by The Actors Centre London. The Lab ran weekly training and rehearsal sessions in London with over 40 ensemble members and produced a pop-up touring production of *The Love of The Nightingale* with a cast of 24.

Rough Fiction is supported by ETT Forge – English Touring Theatre's talent development programme that champions UK touring, and was previously associate company at The Point, Eastleigh. Previous producing and funding partners have included Arts Council England, Brighton Dome and Festival, Newbury Corn Exchange, The Point Eastleigh, London Arts Orchestra, Barbican / Guildhall, Cockayne Grants for The Arts, and The London Community Foundation.

Celia Dugua | General Manager

Celia is a producer based in London, interested in developing new work. Producing credits include: Offie-Nominated *Vincent River* by Philip Ridley (Park Theatre), *Dirty Little Machine* by Miranda Huba, *Rabbits* by Joe Hampson (Park Theatre), Offie-Nominated *Thérèse Raquin* directed by Seb Harcombe (Southwark Playhouse), *Happy to Help* by Michael Ross (Park Theatre), *The Cause* by Jeremy James (Jermyn Street Theatre). Associate credits include: *Dirty Great Love Story* (Arts Theatre – West End), *Dinner with Friends* directed by Tom Attenborough (Park Theatre), *Electric* (Big House Theatre, Rio Cinema).

General Management credits include: *Jellyfish* by Ben Weatherill (Bush Theatre), *Vixen* an immersive re-imagining of Janacek's classic, designed by Daisy Evans and Silent Opera, with support from the English National Opera.

Jane Arnold-Forster | Production Manager

Most recent theatre credits include: *Out of the Cage*, *Thark* (Park Theatre), *Even Stillness Breathes Softly Against a Brick Wall* (The Soho), *Port*, *The Captain of Kopenick* and *This House* (National Theatre), *La Boheme*, *The Man on Her Mind*

(Charing Cross Theatre), *Ignorance* (Hampstead Downstairs), *A Life* (Finborough Theatre), *The Only True History of Lizzie Finn* (Southwark Playhouse).

Kate Eccles | Stage Manager

Theatre includes: *Othello, Paint Your Wagon* (Liverpool Everyman Theatre), *The Box of Delights* (Wilton's Music Hall), *Le Grand Mort* (Trafalgar Studios 2), *My Mother Medea, Jeramee, Hartleby and Oooglemore, The Velveteen Rabbit, Baby Show, Cinderella: A Fairy Tale, Dora* (Unicorn Theatre), *Pop* (Roundhouse), *The Haunting of Hill House, The Match Box, Held* (Liverpool Playhouse), *Hōp* (The London Wonderground Spiegeltent), *The Epic Adventure of Nhamo the Manyika Warrior and His Sexy Wife Chipo* (The Tricycle Theatre), *Molly Wobbly's Tit Factory, The Painkiller, Brendan at the Chelsea, The Crucible* (Lyric Theatre, Belfast), *And A Nightingale Sang* (The New Vic) *Tom's Midnight Garden, Shining City, Stones in his Pockets, Summer Lightning, The Lady in the Van, The Caretaker* (Theatre by the Lake, Keswick)

MENTAL HEALTH PARTNER CHARITIES

Campaign Against Living Miserably (CALM)

The Campaign Against Living Miserably (CALM) is leading a movement against suicide, the single biggest killer of men under 45 in the UK. CALM provides frontline support for men who may be going through a tough time in their life, as well as offering support for those affected by suicide and campaigning for culture change around issues such as mental health, suicide and masculinity.

Every day from 5pm-midnight CALM's free, confidential and anonymous helpline and webchat are available for any man who needs support. Visit www.thecalmzone.net to access information, advice and inspiring stories.

Stuart Low Trust

Stuart Low Trust (SLT) was set up in response to a young man who killed himself as he could not find the support he needed to help him cope with his schizophrenia. SLT is a lifeline for hundreds of vulnerable, socially isolated people, experiencing suicidal thoughts, in poverty and living with mental ill health. We offer safe, inclusive, cohesive, non-judgemental activities, with a core aim of bringing people together and offering companionship. Attendees come from all over London.

Our activities provide a sense of community and mostly happen in evenings and weekends, when people may be at their lowest ebb, with few alternatives. Our Friday evening's offer nutritious food, entertainment or an interesting talk. We offer Saturday workshops, Philosophy, Choir, Garden Club, Art and outings. One attendee wrote: "Being here has liberated my life". Attendees can volunteer, with training and support, so they feel valued. Want to join or support us?

www.slt.org.uk | 020 7713 9304 | info@slt.org.uk

Mind (Haringey)

Mind in Haringey provides information, advice and support to people affected by mental health problems. We work to prevent mental health problems, promote mental wellbeing and ensure those with mental health problems are respected and included in our local community. Our mission is to support anyone in Haringey with mental health issues by listening to people, defending their rights and helping them to lead fulfilling lives.

Our values

- We listen with care, respect and offer reassurance to everyone we encounter.
- We seek to influence and improve mental health services in Haringey, raising awareness and challenging both stigma and discrimination.
- We are committed to easy and equal access for everyone in Haringey.
- We consider opportunities for collaboration when developing services.
- We seek continuous improvement in all we do.

Services we offer include our counselling service and the recently launched Haringey Wellbeing Network.

Mind in Haringey | www.mindinharingey.org.uk

020 8340 2474

Mental Health Crisis Support

Please use the following services if you or someone you know may be experiencing a mental health crisis.

999

If someone is at serious risk of death or injury call 999 and ask for police, fire or ambulance.

Call your GP

Most surgeries have an out of hours phone number, and you should be able to book an emergency appointment.

Contact your Care Co-Ordinator

Or other allocated health professional (e.g. Community Psychiatric Nurse (CPN)).

Go to A&E

If you are worried you may hurt yourself or someone else without help, go to your nearest Accident & Emergency Department.

Contact confidential helplines and sources of support:

Samaritans
08457 90 90 90 (24 hours) | www.samaritans.org

PARYRUS
Prevention of Young Suicide
0800 068 41 41
(Mon-Fri, 10am – 5pm & 7pm – 10pm; weekends 2pm – 5pm)
www.papyrus-uk.org

Campaign Against Living Miserably (CALM)
0800 58 58 58 (7 days a week, 5pm – midnight)
www.thecalmzone.net

SANE
0845 767 8000 (7 days a week, 6pm – 11pm)
www.sane.org.uk

MIND
0300 123 3393 (Mon-Fri, 9am – 6pm)
www.mind.org.uk

Maytree
A sanctuary for the suicidal (based in Finsbury Park).
0207 263 7070
www.maytree.org.uk/index.php

About Park Theatre

Park Theatre was founded by Artistic Director, Jez Bond and Creative Director, Melli Marie. The building opened in May 2013 and, with four West End transfers, two National Theatre transfers and ten national tours in its first five years, quickly garnered a reputation as a key player in the London theatrical scene. Park Theatre has received two Olivier nominations, won an Offie for Best New Play (*The Revlon Girl*) and won The Stage's Fringe Theatre of the Year in 2015.

Park Theatre is an inviting and accessible venue, delivering work of exceptional calibre in the heart of Finsbury Park. We work with writers, directors and designers of the highest quality to present compelling, exciting and beautifully told stories across our two intimate spaces.

Our programme encompasses a broad range of work from classics to revivals with a healthy dose of new writing, producing in-house as well as working in partnership with emerging and established producers. We strive to play our part within the UK's theatre ecology by offering mentoring, support and opportunities to artists and producers within a professional theatre-making environment.

Our Creative Learning strategy seeks to widen the number and range of people who participate in theatre, and provides opportunities for those with little or no prior contact with the arts.

In everything we do we aim to be warm and inclusive; a safe, welcoming and wonderful space in which to work, create and visit.

★★★★★ *"A five-star neighbourhood theatre."* Independent

As a registered charity [number 1137223] with no public subsidy, we rely on the kind support of our donors and volunteers. To find out how you can get involved visit **parktheatre.co.uk**

For Park Theatre
Artistic Director | Jez Bond
Executive Director | Rachael Williams
Creative Director | Melli Marie
Development Director | Dorcas Morgan
Sales & Marketing Director | Dawn James
Sales & Marketing Manager | Rachel McCall
Sales & Marketing Intern | Holly Thompson
Finance Manager | Elaine Lavelle
Finance & Adminstration Officer | Susie Italiano
Development & Production Assistant | Daniel Cooper
Technical & Buildings Manager | Sacha Queiroz
Deputy Technical & Buildings Manager | Neal Gray
Administrator | Melissa Bonnelame
Learning Care & Access Coordinator | Lorna Heap
Interim Venue & Volunteer Manager | Barry Card
Duty Venue Managers | Shaun Joynson, Amy Allen
Head of Food & Beverage | Brett Reynolds
Senior Cafe Bar Manager | Squiff Wordsworth
Bar Staff | Sally Antwi, Victoria Amankwa, Gemma Barnett, Florence Blackmore, Grace Boateng, Calum Budd-Brophy, Robert Czibi, Jack De Deney, Adam Harding-Khair, Philip Honeywell, Matthew Littleson, Matthew McCallion, Jack Mosedale, Ryan Peek, Alice Pegram, Maisie Sadgrove, Mitchell Snell, Sara Vohra
Box Office Supervisors | Sofi Berenger, Celia Dugua, Natasha Green, Holly McCormish, Jack Mosedale, Libby Nash and Alex Whitlock
Public Relations | Nick Pearce and Julie Holman for Target Live

President | Jeremy Bond

Ambassadors
David Horovitch
Celia Imrie
Sean Mathias
Tanya Moodie
Hattie Morahan
Tamzin Outhwaite
Meera Syal

Associate Artist
Mark Cameron

Trustees
Andrew Cleland-Bogle
Nick Frankfort
Robert Hingley
Mars Lord
Sir Frank McLoughlin
Bharat Mehta
Rufus Olins
Nigel Pantling (Chair)
Victoria Phillips
Jo Parker
Leah Schmidt (Vice Chair)

With thanks to all of our supporters, donors and volunteer

DISTANCE

by Alex McSweeney

Characters:

STEVEN

ALAN

SONJA

THE DUKE

FOLAMI / TICKET INSPECTOR / WAITRESS

JASPER: a boy (VOICE ONLY)

AN OPENING

A Chair. Then a MAN sitting. Hands to head. Silent scream. Winter in the mind – wailing. Bacon's middle triptych. Whirligig. Chaos. Confines of a room. He puts his hands out in front of him and makes two firm fists. His whole body tenses into a fist. Knuckle-white strained. Muttering now. Trancelike. Reaches down to a bottle of brandy. Bottle to mouth. Drains it. He lifts his hands to the ceiling for someone. Reaches down. For something. Looks up. Tries to raise himself from the chair...

IN MOTION NOW

Station. Slats up. Smooth floor. Clack, clack. Panting. Tick tock boom. Whistle. Hands up. Orange light. Eyes to time. Clack, clack. Train. Pass through. Clunk. In now. Settle.

STEVEN *sees* ALAN. *Swallow.*

ALAN:	Fuck me.
STEVEN:	Thought it was you.
ALAN:	Fucking hell.
STEVEN:	I was looking at you.
ALAN:	Shit.
STEVEN:	The hair.
ALAN:	How are you?
STEVEN:	I'm all right. I'm all right. Yeah.
ALAN:	You're not up for...?
STEVEN:	Yeah.
ALAN:	You're joking?

STEVEN: Yeah. No...?

ALAN: Yeah, yeah.

STEVEN: Faulkner man?

ALAN: Anything man, within reason. I've dabbled around it. Supporting statement etc.

STEVEN: Always good.

ALAN: They'll put us through it – this lot.

STEVEN: Yes.

ALAN: Fuckers.

Breathe.

STEVEN: (*Looking at his hair*) So what's going on?

ALAN: (*Putting his hand through his hair*) Just growing it.

STEVEN: Looks all right.

ALAN: I'm doing the grey and distinguished. You know – fuller.

STEVEN: Sort of.

ALAN: That's it. Do you have to sit where your ticket says?

STEVEN: Peak time.

ALAN: Where is everybody? Fuck it, I'll sit here for a bit. Never get on these things. Fucking rip off. Hundred and thirty-eight quid! I should be able to sit wherever I like. I should be allowed to sit on the driver's lap.

STEVEN:	You paid a hundred and thirty-eight quid?
ALAN:	What did you pay?
STEVEN:	Did you not book in advance?
ALAN:	No
STEVEN:	Why not?
ALAN:	Couldn't be fucked.
STEVEN:	That'll be it.
ALAN:	What did you pay?
STEVEN:	Sixty-six quid.
ALAN:	You're joking.
STEVEN:	No. I booked a week ago.
ALAN:	Great, I'm a reserver.
STEVEN:	Eh?
ALAN:	I'm reserve shortlist then. Only found out Tuesday.
STEVEN:	Doesn't always work like that.
ALAN:	Yes, it does. (*Beat*) I get it back anyway. The cash. Travel and shit. So, so, so, so. Shit, how long has it been? When did I see you last?
STEVEN:	Think it was... Wasn't it Greenwich?
ALAN:	No, I've seen you since then. That was years ago. Wasn't it? Must have seen you since then.

STEVEN: Don't think so. (*Indicating his sun glasses*) You wearing those all the way?

ALAN: Fair question but I've got this going on.

Takes off his sunglasses.

STEVEN: Jesus. What happened?

ALAN: I do not know.

STEVE: Eh?

ALAN: Got no idea. Honestly, just came up.

STEVEN: Freaky.

ALAN: I know.

STEVEN: You might have sneezed.

ALAN: Someone said that. Might have been on my bike. I might've got something in there or hit it or something. Knocked it with the helmet.

STEVEN: You on a bike?

ALAN: Yeah.

STEVEN: Push?

ALAN: Motor.

STEVEN: What you got?

ALAN: Hornet.

STEVEN: Cc?

ALAN: 600.

STEVEN: Rock 'n' roll.

ALAN:	What's my middle name? (*Beat*) So, how's you and yours?
STEVEN:	Yabba dabba doo.
ALAN:	Great. What does that..? Is that…?
STEVEN:	All fine.
ALAN:	That was convincing.
STEVEN:	No, no.
ALAN:	Alright, mate.
STEVEN:	As it happens – don't worry about it – (*Gesture*)
ALAN:	Shit. What? …How do you mean?
STEVEN:	No nothing.
ALAN:	What?
STEVEN:	No.
ALAN:	Jesus, don't leave me hanging.
STEVEN:	It's fine.
ALAN:	Alright, mate – no probs.

STEVEN – **Breathe. Eye flicker. Blurred, green fields beyond.**

ALAN:	You're not… ill?
STEVEN:	No.
ALAN:	Right.

Leave it. No.

STEVEN: Me and Sonja.

ALAN: No?

STEVEN: Yeah.

ALAN: You're joking!? Are you serious? Fucking hell.

STEVEN: Yeah.

ALAN: Steve.

STEVEN: Mmmm.

ALAN: The best weddings...

STEVEN: They say.

ALAN: What happened... or if you don't want - ?

STEVEN: No, its all right. It's just things.

ALAN: Steve...

STEVEN: That's how. We err.

ALAN: Err?

STEVEN: Yeah.

ALAN: Right. Fucking hell. Did you err?

STEVEN: Not really.

ALAN: Hmm. Who did you...? Did you err? With someone?

STEVEN: I didn't do anything.

ALAN: Eh?

STEVEN: Met a woman at a party.

ALAN: Stay with me, Goose.

STEVEN: We didn't do anything.

ALAN: And Sonja's gone doolally?

STEVEN: Yeah.

ALAN: But you told her…?

STEVEN: Yeah, but its… issues. Ongoing.

ALAN: Jesus. How bad is it?

STEVEN: Bad.

ALAN: Inoperable?

STEVEN: Hard to think beyond.

ALAN: Well, I'm sorry to hear that. I really am, Steve.

STEVEN: Yeah.

Out the window. A quiver. Fluttering. Moths. At the back of the neck.

ALAN: How's Jasper taking it?

STEVEN: He doesn't know what the fuck is going on.

ALAN: Sonja doing a blankety blank or is their dialogue or what's going on?

STEVEN: Daddy's living in a little room round the corner.

ALAN: Okay. Jesus, Steve. But you didn't do anything.

STEVEN: That's Sonja.

ALAN:	What are these creatures?
STEVEN:	(*Gesture*).
TANNOY:	Welcome to 07:50 Virgin service into Manchester Piccadilly. Our estimated arrival time on this journey is 09:58. There is a buffet car at the rear of the train selling a selection of snacks and hot and cold beverages.
ALAN:	When did it all kick off?
STEVEN:	August.
ALAN:	Jesus.
STEVEN:	I know.
ALAN:	Killers.
STEVEN:	There you go.

SHIFT

Table. Two glasses of wine. Tapping into tablets and mobiles.

SONJA:	(*Looking into her phone*) I tell you, Dill and Jay have some weird friends.
STEVEN:	(*Looking into his tablet*) Mmm.
SONJA:	They always post weird freak show photos. Them and their friends. So strange.
STEVEN:	Mmm hm.
SONJA:	They always look the best. Normal. The rest…
STEVEN:	Fat club?
SONJA:	Yep.

STEVEN: (*Tapping into his tablet*) That's why they post them.

SONJA: They must have some normal friends.

STEVEN: It's the country.

SONJA: No.

STEVEN: (*Finishing a thought*) You give up. Babe, (*Into his tablet – tapping*) thesis statement - "For all its infamous violence and transgression, it is towards such a future that…" or "the notion of a future that…"?

SONJA: Last one.

STEVEN: "the notion of a future that…"?

SONJA: Sounds better. Dill looks good.

STEVEN: (*Tapping*) Let's have a look.

SONJA *turns her phone around.*

STEVEN: She looks all right. Fuck me look at that one. That's not a great one of Jay either.

SONJA: He's so lovely.

STEVEN: Nice guy. So wait – (*Reading*) "For all its infamous violence and transgression, the notion of a future that the literature of marginality inaugurated by *Naked Lunch* finally points"?

SONJA: Doesn't make sense.

STEVEN *looks at the tablet.*

SHIFT

ALAN: So, who's this other woman?

STEVEN: (*Looking at tablet*) Nobody.

ALAN: Just a little ding dong?

STEVEN: We didn't have sex.

ALAN: Okay. Student?

STEVE: No. She had four kids.

ALAN: Fuck a duck.

STEVEN: We met at a party. Just texted a bit.

ALAN: Where is your penis?

STEVEN: There's it. Sorry, I forgot to ask, all good with Alice and that?

ALAN: Yes. Sorry to be family fortunes and that but, you know, things are good. Me. Alice and Molly. It's great. And another one on the way.

STEVEN: Shit. Congratulations.

ALAN: Sorry, probably the last thing...

STEVEN: No, No. Good for you. Really.

STEVEN - *Tipping out of the seat. Hurtling. Stone. Through air. Down.*

SHIFT

SONJA: We do need to see them.

STEVEN: (*Reading*) Mmm hm.

31

SONJA:	It's been too long. Gets embarrassing.
STEVEN:	Mmm.
SONJA:	We should invite them.
STEVEN:	Yup.
SONJA:	Do you think?
STEVEN:	Mmm.
SONJA:	What did I just say?
STEVEN:	We should invite them.
SONJA:	What do you think?
STEVEN:	Yes, invite them. (*Beat*) Not that nutter kid of theirs. Babe, help me out.
SONJA:	They can't stay without Bella.
STEVEN:	Count me out. Got to finish this.
SONJA:	Where's she going to stay?
STEVEN:	Basement. Babe, please – this is for tomorrow – I just need a normal human's ear – so not "the notion of a future that…" – I'll do "towards". (*Tapping into tablet*). So… "For all its infamous violence and transgression, it is towards such a future that the literature of marginality inaugurated by *Naked Lunch* finally points"?
SONJA:	Perfect.
STEVEN:	Yes? Make sense?
SONJA:	Yes. Clever clogs.

A WAITRESS *comes over with an electronic order pad.*

WAITRESS: Are you ready to order?

Putting phones down.

        STEVEN: Sorry, we haven't even looked yet.

Together:

        SONJA: Sorry sorry just a few minutes.

WAITRESS: No problem. I can come back.

STEVEN: Yes. Are there any specials?

WAITRESS: Everything's fairly special in so much as it's a locally sourced menu. It's a provenance menu – changes every day. Do you need me to go through any of it with you?

STEVEN: No, that's fine. We'll have a look.

WAITRESS *shoots* STEVEN *a smile.*

WAITRESS: Ok, I'll be back in five.

STEVEN: Great.

STEVEN *watches her go.*

STEVEN: Provenance menu suck my cock.

SONJA: Shhhh. What are you having?

STEVEN: Don't know. Can't decide duck or steak.

SONJA: Might have two starters.

STEVEN: (*Reaching over and touching her belly tenderly*) Have something proper.

SONJA: Or maybe the sole. Caper butter.

STEVEN: Don't have fish.

SONJA: Eh?

STEVEN: You shouldn't have fish in a restaurant.

SONJA: Is that Steven logic?

STEVEN: No. Fish is fish. It should be out of the sea and on the plate. Don't muck about with it.

SONJA: Caper butter's not mucking about.

STEVEN: No, I mean fish doesn't need anything. We can do fish. Or you can. You do fish.

SONJA: I just fancy it.

STEVEN: Okay. I'll have the steak. I can never get it right at home.

SONJA: Have the steak. (*Beat*) Though you have mussels all the time. In restaurants.

STEVEN: They're not fish. They're crustaceans. And *you* can't eat those now.

SONJA: You look like a crustacean. In the morning. (*Beat*) They're molluscs though, aren't they?

STEVEN: Not necessarily.

SONJA: Is that you being you?

STEVEN: They can be considered molluscs or crustaceans.

SONJA: Really.

STEVEN: Yes/No.

They laugh. The WAITRESS *returns.* STEVEN *smiles at her.* SONJA *watches* STEVEN *watching the* WAITRESS.

WAITRESS: Hi.

STEVEN: We're decisive. I'll have the steak.

WAITRESS: Which one?

STEVEN: (*Scrambling back to the menu*) The...the...I'll have the...rib-eye. Yes. Medium please.

      ALAN: So, this woman. The other one.

WAITRESS: For madam?

SONJA: Sole.

      ALAN: You didn't do anything. Meet at a party.

WAITRESS: (*Inputting*) <u>Sole</u>.   Troubled <u>soul</u>. Few drinks downed.

WAITRESS: Any sides?

      ALAN: Numbers exchanged.
SONJA: No, we're fine <u>thanks</u>. <u>Thanks.</u> Naughty but nice. Silly arse stuff. Sonja finds the texts...

The WAITRESS *departs.*

SONJA: I'll text Dill.

STEVEN: (*To both*) Yeah.

SONJA: We'll put something in for September.

35

STEVEN: Yeah. Some emails.

SHIFT

ALAN: Emails?

STEVEN: Yeah.

ALAN: You said it was texts.

STEVEN: Texts, Emails. Same thing. Communication.

ALAN: Emails.

STEVEN: Yeah, communication.

ALAN: Well… no. I mean, texts is a stupid arse thing when you're pissed and that. But emails… you know.

STEVEN: Same thing.

ALAN: Facebook stuff?

STEVEN: No, email.

ALAN: Right.

STEVEN: Normal emails.

ALAN: Right.

STEVEN: Look, there were things beforehand.

ALAN: Okay.

STEVEN: Should have been dealt with.

ALAN: Okay. Going back? What… since Jasper or…?

STEVEN: And other things.

ALAN: Right.

Beat.

STEVEN: (*Opening his holdall and pulling out some notes*) Look, I should probably have a look at this. Go through it a bit.

ALAN: Sure. Absolutely. Me too.

STEVEN – *Scratching around in the neck, then head – pats around the top of the head – then to the side - searching - wants put his hands in and lift his brain out. Stare at it. Pull a bit off and put the brain back. Gently circling a spot of his skull by the frontal lobe.*

ALAN: What time you in?

STEVEN: Twelve-thirty.

ALAN: Presentation?

STEVEN: Yeah.

ALAN: Interview?

STEVEN: Four-thirty.

ALAN: Right.

STEVEN: You?

ALAN: Eleven and three.

STEVEN: You'll have to peg it.

ALAN: I know. (*Beat*) You got hard copies, there? For the presentation?

STEVEN: Yeah.

ALAN: For the panel?

STEVEN: Yeah. You powerpointing?

ALAN: No. People are sick of fucking powerpoints. Boring as a dog's arse.

STEVEN: Hard copying?

ALAN: No, I've got one – some – one – but I'm just referring to it. Going impro.

STEVEN: Bold.

ALAN: Fucking cheek. Come up with a whole module on Faulkner's narrative technique!!!! I'm going to riff on the theme. (*Beat*) Can I have a quick butchers?

STEVEN: No.

ALAN: (*Looking over* STEVEN's *work*) You powerpointing as... What's all this? Faulkner – The Ironies of Southern Identity, *Sound and The Fury* – Modernist Odyssey, Character as Omniscient... Have you? This is the whole module.

STEVEN: Yes.

ALAN: You've done the whole module?

STEVEN: It's what they want. What they expect.

ALAN: Steve, this is too... Why are you going for this?

STEVEN: Space.

ALAN: Right.

STEVEN: Different space.

ALAN: Of course. Would you actually take it?

STEVEN: Don't know.

ALAN: Well, leave it to the desperate cunts, will you. Shit, better have a look at this now.

STEVEN *laughs.*

STEVEN – *Swimming now. Blue. Arclight. Shudder at the back of neck. Moths scratching. Gasping. Trying to take in more air. Sinking... into the blue.*

Time is stretched. Things are slow and muffled.

ALAN: So, these emails. I mean, what sort of stuff was in them?

STEVEN: Emails.

ALAN: What was in these emails?

STEVEN: Emails.

ALAN: Steven? What was in the emails?

STEVEN: Nothing.

ALAN: Dirty stuff?

STEVEN: No. More...

ALAN: Oh, no. Not my wife doesn't understand me shit?

STEVEN: More along those lines.

ALAN: Fucking hell.

STEVEN – *The carriage begins to shift around. It gently begins to spin. Speech becomes clearer and faster.*

STEVEN: She was the same. We talked to each other. Sonja and I...

ALAN: Well, least you didn't do the dirty or anything. There might still be a way back. You never know. A few emails, intent but not acted upon. No fluids exchanged.

STEVEN: That's not how Sonja sees it.

ALAN: Previous?

STEVEN: Not really. Nothing major.

ALAN: A few emails won't stand up in court.

STEVEN: We met a few times.

ALAN: You met?

STEVEN: A few times.

The carriage is spinning faster now.

ALAN: You met a few times? Where?

STEVEN: We had lunch.

ALAN: Fucking hell, Steve.

STEVEN: We had lunch a couple of times.

ALAN: Jesus.

STEVEN: Nothing happened. We just talked. That was it.

ALAN: And then you bummed her in the toilet?

STEVEN: It wasn't like that.

Faster now. Spinning. Whirlpool. The tank is emptying.

ALAN: Pink penny, brown penny. Pink penny, brown penny.

STEVEN: Nothing like that.

ALAN: I'm sorry. I'm only joking. So you just talked.

STEVEN: She was going through a time – so was I.

ALAN: And Sonja finds out.

STEVEN: Yeah.

ALAN: Right. Jesus, Steve. This is a whole world of mess, this is.

STEVEN: I know.

Spinning wildly now. Whirligig down the plug hole and STEVEN *is*

SHOT OUT

Into - Pretend bullshit of domestic living. Veneer. SONJA waits.

STEVEN: (*Soaking wet*) Cats and dogs. Hey, honey.

SONJA: Hey.

STEVEN *goes over and kisses her. She is cold.*

STEVEN: (*Taking his drenched clothes off*) All good?

SONJA: Hm?

STEVEN: All good? Your day?

SONJA: Sure. Why wouldn't it be?

STEVEN: Eh?

SONJA: Why wouldn't it be a good day?

STEVEN: I don't know. I was just asking.

SONJA: Just asking?

STEVEN:	What?
SONJA:	Just happy old asking your idiot wife?
STEVEN:	What!? What's wrong!?
SONJA:	What's wrong he asks the fool.
STEVEN:	Sorry, what's...? Have I done something?
SONJA:	Have you done something? Have you done something!?
STEVEN:	Sorry, what's going on?
SONJA:	You tell me.
STEVEN:	Sorry, I'm a bit lost here...
SONJA:	Just "touching base", loverboy.
STEVEN:	What?!
SONJA:	Just checking how things are "back at the ranch", cowboy.
STEVEN:	You're fucking nuts!
SONJA:	Sure I am. I am nuts.
STEVEN:	Look, will you just tell me...?
SONJA:	Check your email.
STEVEN:	Eh?
SONJA:	Check your email. I have.
STEVEN:	My email?
SONJA:	Yeah, the fucking thing you spend half your life on.

STEVEN *freezes.*

SONJA: "Barrier's up here. No change there" – "keep passing open doors" – "things should be confronted but…" – "thinks we just need a break" – "drifts in and out" – "cornflakes and see you tonight". Add your own violin, you cock.

STEVEN *motionless. Silence.*

                      ALAN: You doing the lunch?

STEVEN: Hmm?

                      ALAN: You signed up for the lunch?

STEVEN: For the –

SONJA: What did you have for <u>lunch</u>?   . ALAN: <u>Lunch</u>

STEVEN: For lunch?

SONJA: Lunch, dear. Lunch. The one after breakfast.

STEVEN: Er…

SONJA: What did she have?

STEVEN: I'm…

SONJA: Did you have a pasta? I bet you did. A carbonara? A juicy fat carbonara. Did the cream dribble down your fat fucking face? What about her? Just a salad? Little dainty little salad, was it?

STEVEN: Sonja…

SONJA: Where was it? Oh, that's it, *Ida*'s wasn't it? 1pm but I might be a bit late. That's okay, I'll wait.

STEVEN *sits and puts his head in his hands.*

SONJA: That's it, sit down. You must be exhausted after all that fucking. Sit down –

STEVEN: It's not like that…

SONJA: No, no. Sit down and relax. We don't want you over-exerting yourself again. Not twice in a day. Or maybe you did it a few times, did you? In the restaurant? In the toilet? Maybe on the table? Don't mind us, we're just getting it while we can! We can't help it. There's two fucking idiots at home but we just can't keep our hands off each other.

STEVEN: Sonja…

SONJA: Ah, poor misunderstood hubby. Nobody to talk to. Really *talk* to. Nobody…

STEVEN: Where's Jasper?

SONJA: At Sarah's. What's it to you? Not all of a sudden a family man?

No answer. SONJA *glares at the still seated* STEVEN.

SONJA: So, no answer?!!! NO FUCKING ANSWER!

SONJA *launches herself at* STEVEN. *She hits him repeatedly.* STEVE *remains seated covering his head.*

SONJA: (*Each word a punch*) YOU – HAVE – TO – FUCK – UP – EVER - YTHING – YOU – HAVE – TO – FUCK - ING – RUIN – EVERY – FUCK – ING – THING – …

Suddenly STEVEN *launches himself at* SONJA *and grabs her violently by the throat.*

STEVEN: WE NEVER HAD ANYTHING YOU FUCKING BITCH!!! WE HAVEN'T GOT ANYTHING!!!!

STEVEN *throws her violently on to the floor.* SONJA *realigns herself and in one move gets up and picks up a mug from the coffee table and hurls it at him. It misses.*

STEVEN: That could have killed me!

SONJA: I hope you drown in your own blood.

SONJA *busts into uncontrollable sobs and crumples to the floor. After a moment* STEVE *begins to go to her. Before it is more than a thought,* SONJA *spits out…*

SONJA: Don't…

Silence. SONJA *on the floor and* STEVEN *standing some feet away.* STEVEN *sits. Silence.*

SONJA: Get out of this house.

                      ALAN: The union should know this. Prepare basically their whole unit for a semester. What are you doing?

STEVEN: *The Sound and the Fury.*

STEVEN *heads for the door.*

SONJA: There he goes. That simple.

                           ALAN: Don't really know that one.

STEVEN: Wouldn't let on about that.

SONJA: Thought I'd wait for the face. Just to see. And there it was. Get out.

STEVEN: It's not...

SONJA: Fuck off.

He does.

SHIFT

ALAN: I do mention it. In passing.

STEVEN: Okay.

ALAN: Unwise?

STEVEN: If you don't know it don't mention it. Not that one. Take it out altogether. What are you doing?

ALAN: *The Reivers.*

STEVEN: Okay.

ALAN: Bad choice?

STEVEN: Not necessarily.

ALAN: Look Steve, I know you're not sure if you want this job but I really do. In fact, I need this job. So, if there is any way you could assist me in not fucking it up, I would be grateful. You think I should take out the reference to *Sound and Fury*.

STEVEN: Have you read it?

ALAN: All of it?

STEVEN: Yes.

ALAN: No.

STEVEN: Then take it out. What are you focusing on?

ALAN: Point of view.

STEVEN: You should be fine with *The Reivers*.

ALAN: Yeah?

STEVEN: With *Absolom!* or *Dying* they'll want interior monologue and stream of consciousness. Or they'll go cinematic montage effect and free, lyric language.

ALAN: I might just jot some of this down.

STEVEN: What are you like on the others?

ALAN: Of the...?

STEVEN: Yes, have you read any of his other novels?

ALAN: No. (*Beat*) Fuck's sake. I can do a twenty minute presentation on Faulkner's fucking narrative technique.

STEVEN – *A shudder.*

STEVEN: Still falling.

ALAN: What more do they want?

STEVEN: If I fade it'll be on them.

ALAN: Steve?

STEVEN: I'm under their feet.

ALAN: Who?

STEVEN: I'm under their fate. My fate.

ALAN: Steve? Are you alright?

STEVEN: If they think I'll go then they'll think it.

ALAN: Go? Where? Steve, are you alright?

STEVEN - *A shudder. Scratching. Branches and leaves at the back of the head. Scurrying mice. Takes out a small mirror from his pocket – raises it – looks up into it to look at the top of his head. An opening – a door – to reach into the top of his head and put his hands in and lift his brain out again. Study it. Shake it. Pull two chunks off and put the brain back. Small circles – frontal lobe – gently.*

ALAN: Steve? What are you...?

MAN: Gentlemen, greetings.

A MAN with a guitar over his shoulder is there.

MAN: (*Indicating the table and seats opposite*) Are these seats, to your knowledge, taken?

ALAN: Not as far as we know.

MAN: Obliged in many ways.

The MAN sits at the adjacent table seat.

MAN: Are these seats allocated, my friend?

ALAN: Not to our knowledge.

MAN: These are dangerous days.

ALAN: Are they?

MAN: You know. I see.

STEVEN and ALAN look at each other.

MAN: (*Sitting*) Things begin and end.

ALAN: They do.

STEVEN: That's a fact.

MAN: We are one. I am the Duke.

ALAN: The Duke?

THE DUKE: That's what they call me.

ALAN: Nice to meet you, Duke.

STEVEN: Likewise.

THE DUKE: They'll get us all, the cunts. In the end.

ALAN: Yes.

THE DUKE: But we shall fight, shall we not?

ALAN: Let's hope so.

THE DUKE: What brings you this way, men?

ALAN: Business type things.

THE DUKE: Ah, these are things for these days. And what of you, quiet one?

STEVEN: The same, basically.

THE DUKE: Business is for people who make business when business is necessary. Now is not such a time.

ALAN: That's right.

THE DUKE: Do you have tickets, my friends?

ALAN: Tickets?

THE DUKE: Yes.

ALAN: For the train?

THE DUKE: For this train.

ALAN: Yes.

THE DUKE: I do not. They shall come for me. In time.

ALAN: You don't have a ticket?

THE DUKE: What is a ticket? A piece of paper that permits me this and that at some others' pleasure.

STEVEN's *eyes become a kaleidoscope which fix on* THE DUKE.

THE DUKE: You are with us, the quiet one. I see.

ALAN: Do they have ticket people, you know inspector jobbies on trains nowadays?

STEVEN: They do.

THE DUKE: We will be ready, will we not?

ALAN: Yes... but we have tickets, to let you know.

THE DUKE: The ticket is but a slip of paper but we are one. Yes?

ALAN: Yes. We probably are, in a way.

STEVEN: Where are you from, Duke?

THE DUKE: Many places. (*Beat*) Do either of you have a smoke? I am out.

STEVEN: I don't smoke.

ALAN: I don't think you can smoke on these trains. They're sealed.

THE DUKE: Do not concern yourself with what is prohibited by others.

STEVEN *looks / smiles.* ALAN *uneasy.*

THE DUKE: (*Rummaging through his shoulder bag*) I have some emergency stock for such occasions.

THE DUKE *begins to roll a cigarette – the precision of a master.*

ALAN: Duke, you know you can't just stick your head out the window on these trains. They're sealed.

THE DUKE: (*Over*) Pitta patta pitta patta pitta patta pitta patta, the noise of the cunts. Barking orders. Pay them no mind, the rule makers. Guards?! Guarding what? Inspectors?! Inspect my arse!

STEVEN: Duke…

THE DUKE: Speak, quiet one.

STEVEN'*s eyes are connected to* THE DUKE'*s in a coloured beam of light reflecting the outside world in motion through the window.*

STEVEN: Where have you…… been, Duke?

THE DUKE: In other places. Older worlds. Mythical places. There was a festival. There. Of trance, of rave, of jungle, dub, grime. And other things. A festival of the people. I was living in a tree. The holed out trunk of a tree. Thousands of years old. The elders offered me this tree in recognition. They made a sacrifice. To me. Slaughtered a goat and to respect the Gods. We began something.

STEVEN: What happened?

THE DUKE: Trouble twice, friend. When they come, they come. A woman I took to the tree and there bedded her. A woman of salted honey whose skin glowed like satin in the moonlight. Unbeknownst to me she was acopulating with another. Who took unkindly towards me. They closed us down. To never return.

ALAN: So... you were deported?

THE DUKE: A biblical stoning and on to the ferry. Anger is an energy.

STEVEN: So... what are you doing... now? If you don't mind me asking.

THE DUKE: I come and go mostly. Could either of you sponsor me for refreshment at this time of pecuniary hardship for myself?

ALAN: What do you want? Cup of tea?

THE DUKE: Perhaps. Or perhaps something with more growl?

ALAN: It's half eight in the morning. I'm not sure if they'll be serving alcohol.

STEVEN: (*Pulling out his wallet and taking out a five pound note*) Here you are, Duke. Have a drink on me.

THE DUKE *reaches over to take the note. He lingers and smells* STEVEN.

THE DUKE: Obliged to you, good man.

THE DUKE *folds up the note and puts it his trouser pocket.*

THE DUKE:	(*Looking at* STEVE) Troubles.
STEVEN:	Hm?
THE DUKE:	Troubles. Yes?
ALAN:	He's... not had a great time of late.
STEVEN:	It's all right.
THE DUKE:	*I* see. Where things lie.
ALAN:	He's having a few...
STEVEN:	It's okay, Alan.
ALAN:	Relationship stuff...
THE DUKE:	Ah, the softer sex. Has one left the ship between ports?
STEVEN:	It's a bit...
THE DUKE:	Understood. Many of them are cunts. Did she fornicate with another as many of them do?
ALAN:	Other way around...
STEVEN:	No...
THE DUKE:	Ah, you took your meat and fish when it was on the table.

ALAN *laughs*.

STEVEN:	It wasn't really...
THE DUKE:	Yes, yes.
STEVEN:	So where...?
ALAN:	Where you living now, Duke?

THE DUKE:	Croydon. At my birth giver's.
ALAN:	Right. Is that your mum's?
THE DUKE:	At this time.
ALAN:	Right.
THE DUKE:	The bosom of the family is a comforting one. And she does my laundry.
ALAN:	So, how do you survive?
THE DUKE:	At the generosity of the state as is my right as a citizen. I'm at Croydon College in the evenings.
STEVEN:	What are you studying?
THE DUKE:	Creative Writing and Gardening.
ALAN:	Hedging your bets. Wise.
THE DUKE:	If you are a-signing on, you only pay ten per cent. The other estudiantes are paying hundreds. (*Looking down the carriage*) I see by the reflection in my golden eye that a uniformed one is approaching from yon a-joining carriage so I must depart (*Getting up*) I shall reside in the shitter till he has passed. Sinners, let us go down to the river and pray. Bon voyage, my brothers.

THE DUKE *makes his way swiftly down the carriage. Pause.*

ALAN:	Fuck me. What was he all about?
STEVEN:	The Duke.
ALAN:	Was he real?
STEVEN:	It's real...

ALAN: Living at his mum's after all that.

STEVEN: He's alive.

ALAN: The epic and the mundane. Scrounger? Steve?

STEVEN: Living in a tree.

STEVEN – *Dazzled – a glittering stone ahead. Reaching.*

SHIFT

School. Exiting.

SONJA: We'll have to come back with something.

STEVEN: Honestly, we don't need to worry about this. He's had a thing and it's not a big one.

SONJA: She's basically said that he's –

STEVEN: No, he's gone in with a bunch of them and they've had a ruffle a bit. Boys' stuff. He's not... he jumps in with a couple of them.

SONJA: I don't like it.

STEVEN: No. Sure. I don't. We could take him out. If you want?

SONJA: I think so.

STEVEN: It's not a big deal. We... or I could just pick him up early on Thursdays.

SONJA: Could you?

STEVEN: I could. We'll pull him out. I'll pick him up on Thursdays.

SONJA: Can you? I wouldn't get here in time.

STEVEN: I'll do it. I'll talk to Joy.

SONJA: Can you? Thanks.

STEVEN: I'll talk to Joy. I'll make a point.

SONJA: So they know we're taking it seriously. He only really likes it when you're watching anyway.

STEVEN: You know its not Jasper? He's on the side – and freezing his nuts off.

SONJA: I know but I don't like it.

STEVEN: No. (*Beat*) Least his maths is going great guns.

SONJA: It is. That's great. Have you been doing that?

STEVEN: Yeah, we've been doing the whole thing – Mathletics. He loves it.

SONJA: That's good. Great.

STEVEN: (*In*) I could do some extras at mine on a week day? Once. One evening. After school. Or once every two weeks? Something? Or Thursday?

Beat.

SONJA: (*At her car. Takes out her key fob. Presses it*) Bloody things not working.

STEVEN: Hold your finger down.

SONJA: It doesn't work.

STEVEN: Give it here. (*Takes it and points it at the car. No joy. Repeats*) Needs re-programming. It's a fix.

SONJA: How's that work?

STEVEN: They just re-programme the code. It's a fix. They just fuck about with it and charge you.

SONJA: How do I get in? I've got to pick Jasper up from Sarah's.

STEVEN: There's a key in the fob.

SONJA: (*Looking at the key like a chimp on a computer*) Eh?

STEVEN: Yeah. Pull apart the doo dah and there's a key in there. You've got to open the passenger side and be quick cos the alarm goes of. Then stick the key in the ignition sharpish and its sorted.

STEVEN *takes the key back.*

STEVEN: Ready?

SONJA: Yes, you can.

Half a moment. Of them.

STEVEN *pulls the fob apart to reveal the key. He sticks the key in the passenger door and opens it. A piercing alarm sounds.* SONJA *grabs the key from* STEVEN *and rushes round to the driver's side. They laugh.*

She leaves. He's left alone. In the car park. Brake lights disappear.

STEVEN *looks through dappled sunlight as the pendulum of a swing wipes across the yellow/orange rays.* SONJA's *face glides forward and recedes. He holds the rope taught. They laugh. They kiss. In the eyes. He lets her go and she swings back through the sunlight.*

TICKET INSPECTOR: Tickets please.

STEVEN *watches* SONJA *fade in and out of the sun's rays.*

TICKET INSPECTOR: Tickets please. Sir.

STEVEN *smiles – reaching out his hand to touch the arching* SONJA.

TICKET INSPECTOR: Sir? Tickets?

ALAN: Steve?

Out of the sun STEVEN reaches into his pocket and hands the woman his ticket. The TICKET INSPECTOR looks at it before clicking a hole in it.

An ecrands seconds – a visual construction – a fragmented screen within which – STEVEN watches SONJA glide in and out of a splintering sun sky – touching her ankle – moving within the pendulum arc. Continuous throughout below.

ALAN *has begun to franticly rummage around in all his pockets for his ticket. He pulls things out of his pockets; tissues, keys, money. He then rummages through his bag.*

ALAN: Where the hell is it? I just bought the fucking thing.

The TICKET INSPECTOR *waits patiently saying nothing.*

ALAN: (*To the* TICKET INSPECTOR) Sorry, I have got one. Somewhere. What the hell have I done with it? I definitely bought one. It was a hundred and thirty-eight quid. Can you believe that? A hundred and thirty-eight quid.

TICKET INSPECTOR: Did you book in advance, sir?

ALAN: No. (*Checking his top pocket*) Ah, here it is. Thank God. I thought I was going nuts. (*Holding four tickets*) Which one do you need? Why do we need so many?

The TICKET INSPECTOR *takes all four.*

TICKET INSPECTOR: (*Checking the tickets*) I just need to see your journey out.

ALAN: Do you not think a hundred and thirty-eight quid is excessive?

TICKET INSPECTOR: As I say, sir, if you book in advance, it's considerably cheaper.

The ecrands seconds highlight by turns – reflecting then unreflecting – STEVEN *and* SONJA, *then through a prism –* JASPER *looks through a spy-hole laughing, then* ALAN *and The* TICKET INSPECTOR.

ALAN: So, it's a penalising system?

TICKET INSPECTOR: Pardon

ALAN: You're penalised for spontaneity.

TICKET INSPECTOR: It's cheaper if you book in advance, sir.

ALAN: I know that. Spontaneous or indecisive people are punished.

TICKET INSPECTOR: It gives the customer choice, sir. Book early / save money. Book late / be spontaneous/pay more. By the way, sir, this ticket is for carriage D.

ALAN: Yes?

TICKET INSPECTOR: This is carriage C.

ALAN: I know. I'm just sitting with a friend.

TICKET INSPECTOR: (*Indicating a small LED sign above*) This seat is, in fact, pre-booked, sir.

ALAN: Well, there's nobody here, is there?

TICKET INSPECTOR: Not at this stage.

ALAN: There you are then.

TICKET INSPECTOR: They might be getting on at the next stop.

STEVEN – *Swing, swing. Caress.*

ALAN: Well, I'll move when they get here. Or perhaps I'll ask them if they don't mind sitting over there or something as I've run into an old friend. Anyway, the next stop is Stockport or something and that's miles away.

TICKET INSPECTOR: Stoke on Trent, sir. ETA 09.20 at Stoke on Trent. One of the many advantages of pre-booking is reserving your preferred seat of choice. Guaranteed. The next customer will be expecting it, sir.

ALAN: And he shall receive it.

TICKET INSPECTOR: See that he does.

ALAN: What!!!???

TICKET INSPECTOR: I shall have to insist upon it, sir. It is his right. His pre-booked right to get his pre-booked seat. I'll check back later.

ALAN: I've just told you I'll move. What's the bloody problem?

TICKET INSPECTOR: No need for language, sir. I'll turn a blind eye on this occasion.

ALAN: (*To* STEVEN) Is she joking?

STEVEN: (*Half-connecting – to the* TICKET INSPECTOR) It'll be fine. Thank you.

TICKET INSPECTOR: (*Moving on*) Thank you, sir.

ALAN: I need to get off this train. This train is insane.

STEVEN *is still watching the brake lights disappear out the window – an ecrands seconds with the swinging SONJA in dappled light.* SONJA *swings away and doesn't return*

ALAN *senses.*

ALAN: Fuck, I couldn't do this journey again. Would you get a place up here?

STEVEN: Don't know.

ALAN: Could you go up and down? Few nights there, few nights –

STEVEN: Boxes are all the same. Up there down here. No difference.

STEVEN – **Knuckles on wood. Tap tap.**

ALAN: Hey mate – this could be a little kick. What you need.

STEVEN: One box as good as another.

ALAN: Don't go over-thinking stuff. That's reflecting on reflection and reflection. And you fucked up. That's it.

STEVEN: What's the longest you've spent in a room? One room.

ALAN: You mean…?

STEVEN: Not left it. Just stayed in that room. Just you… and the walls.

ALAN: I don't know. A day or two.

STEVEN: Eight days. Not seeing one person or hearing a real voice. You're screaming inside but there's no noise. And you don't speak to anyone and you don't want to speak to anyone.

Tap tap. Knocking again.

ALAN: It's the Shopenhauer thing, I think. Yes. Isn't it?

STEVEN: Eh?

ALAN: You know. What is it? We actually long for solitude because contact with other people pisses us off, causes us pain but solitude drives us towards people because we'd go insane without some contact. It's the distance between us. The optimum distance.

STEVEN: The distance.

ALAN: Yes.

STEVEN: Do you know what will kill you quicker than heroin, cocaine, pills, anything? Brandy. Brandy will kill you quicker than any of them.

ALAN: Steve...

Tap tap. Knock knock.

STEVEN - *Hands to his head.*

Knock knock.

Room. Chair. Brandy.

STEVEN - *Again a white-knuckled fist. Prising apart fingers to squeeze through and stand.*

STEVEN: Come in.

FOLAMI: (*Entering*) Thank you.

STEVEN: It's a bit untidy.

FOLAMI: That's okay.

STEVEN: I don't have many guests.

FOLAMI: Don't worry.

FOLAMI *stands in the middle of the room.*

STEVEN: Had any luck today?

FOLAMI: Excuse me?

STEVEN: Have you managed to get in anywhere? Have you managed to get a foot in the door today?

FOLAMI: We've spoken to some people.

STEVEN: We?

FOLAMI: We've been calling on people today. On this road. Reaching out.

STEVEN: It's not easy to get in, is it? It's a Godless society. Don't you think?

FOLAMI: People have busy lives.

STEVEN: I suppose Mammonism is the great religion now, isn't it? Wouldn't you say? Sorry, you are...?

FOLAMI: Folami.

STEVEN: (*Shaking her hand*) Steven. Are you always on

	your own?
FOLAMI:	We have friends. Brethren on this road.
STEVEN:	Do you think we now worship the God of Mammon? (*Beat*) Can I offer you some tea?
FOLAMI:	No, thank you.
STEVEN:	(*Holding out his hand*) Right. Let's have a look at this then.

FOLAMI *hands him a small book.*

STEVEN:	(*Reading the cover*) 'Finding Peace Within - The Way to Christ', "a book for people in need…". (*Beat*) You're in luck.
FOLAMI:	What do you need?
STEVEN:	What are you offering?
FOLAMI:	Well, many things… salvation.
STEVEN:	Salvation? In the form of…?
FOLAMI:	'The Way'.
STEVEN:	Could you be more specific?
FOLAMI:	Everyone has their own path.
STEVEN:	Sounded simpler at the door. (*Beat*) Where are your friends?

Beat.

| FOLAMI: | (*Holding up another book*) They are here. It's simpler… clearer… with this. |

STEVEN *takes the book.*

| STEVEN: | (*Reading the cover*) 'Why Jesus?'. This one's a |

	lot shorter. This must be the quicker way to… 'The Way'.
FOLAMI:	It's clearer if you follow ACTS.
STEVEN:	Acts?
FOLAMI:	Yes. ACTS. If you start to speak to God every day, it can guide you. A.C.T.S. ACTS: A – Adoration, C – Confession, T – Thanksgiving, S – Supplication. ACTS.
STEVEN:	Thank you. That's much clearer now. I don't want to piss on anybody's alter here but would you mind if we skip back a bit. To the Salvation bit.
FOLAMI:	You're angry, aren't you, Steven?
STEVEN:	Am I?
FOLAMI:	Yes. Why don't we try and find out what's causing your anger?
STEVEN:	No. Why don't we try and find out what answers you're offering?
FOLAMI:	We're offering some solace. Guidance.
STEVEN:	Are you sure you don't want some tea?
FOLAMI:	No, thank you.
STEVEN:	Something stronger?
FOLAMI:	No, thank you.
STEVEN:	You don't mind if I do, do you?

STEVEN *picks up a bottle of brandy at the side of the bed and downs a large draught.* FOLAMI *looks uneasy.* STEVEN *remains standing with the bottle in his hand.*

STEVEN: (*Beginning to pace around the room*) Okay. So... you're here and you're here to stay. To guide. So let's start – the quest for God can be likened to a blind man in a darkened room looking for a black cat that isn't there. Discuss.

FOLAMI *looks uneasily at him.*

STEVEN: No? How about: The study of Theology, as it stands in Christian churches, is the study of nothing; it is founded on nothing; it rests on no principles; it proceeds by no authorities; it has no data; it can demonstrate nothing; and it admits of no conclusion. Discuss.

FOLAMI: Why don't we talk about you?

STEVEN: Why didn't they let James write the Gospel of Jesus the *man*?

Silence.

FOLAMI *begins to edge towards the door.*

STEVEN: You said we were in for the long haul. You said you weren't going to cut out on me.

FOLAMI: I am. I think a colleague can help you.

STEVEN: I'm looking for answers from *you*.

FOLAMI: We need to ask questions before we can give answers.

Beat.

STEVEN: You're a lot better than I thought you'd be.

FOLAMI: How long have you been living here?

STEVEN: Six months.

FOLAMI: Why?

STEVEN: Why? Because my wife left me and took my child and is living in my house that I still have to pay for.

Silence. STEVEN *turns away.*

FOLAMI: Shall we talk about your wife.

STEVEN *turns suddenly on her.*

STEVEN: YOU WATCH YOUR FUCKING MOUTH! YOU FUCKING BITCH! FUCK YOU!

Beat.

FOLAMI: I'm going to leave now, Steven.

STEVEN: No.

STEVEN *walks to the door. He turns the bottle around – holding it by the neck. An oblique threat. He stands in front of the door.*

STEVEN: I need some answers.

FOLAMI: You are behaving in a threatening way, Steven.

STEVEN: You said… you were staying.

FOLAMI: I'm going to get you help.

STEVEN: No. You said…

FOLAMI: I can get someone who can help.

STEVEN: You said… you were… you were…

FOLAMI: I will bring someone, Steven.

STEVEN: You said...

FOLAMI: Steven, I'd like to leave now.

STEVEN *slowly moves to one side.* FOLAMI *cautiously moves towards the door.* STEVEN *moves to the other side of the room.* FOLAMI *is at the door.*

STEVEN: You'll bring someone...

FOLAMI: Yes.

FOLAMI *exits.* STEVEN *is left. Alone. In the room. A motor starts. The walls begin to close in.* STEVEN *breathes. The motor gets louder.*

SHIFT

Through the piercing motor – STEVEN *sees* ALAN *sitting opposite eating half a sandwich and working on his laptop, occasionally deleting and typing etc.*

ALAN: Sorry, Steve. I know you're working but do you think I can just ask you a quick thing?

STEVEN: Yep?

ALAN: If I'm going down the point of view / characterisation route with this. Do you think I can mention the Compsons in passing ie. psychological depth of character, without them questioning it? Or. Or just cut it out but fuck up the flow?

STEVEN: Are you doing Sartorises and Snopeses?

ALAN: In what context?

STEVEN: Traditionalist's view.

ALAN: I'm not touching that.

STEVEN: What were you thinking of touching?

ALAN: You know, little bit about Benjy's psychological complexity.

STEVEN: Told by an idiot?

ALAN: That sort of thing.

STEVEN: Stick with Boon Hoggenback.

ALAN: Yeah?

STEVEN: I would. You can do a lot with that.

ALAN: Yeah? (*Beat*) Help me out a bit, Steve. I'm struggling.

STEVEN: Frame it with acknowledged responses to Faulkner's characterisation. Dialogue / language is where you want to be heading.

ALAN: Yeah.

ALAN *begins typing into his laptop.*

STEVEN: Jason's language reveals his character straight away: "Once a bitch always a bitch, what I say". Jason *is* the fury. The frustrations of young neurotic men. Hatred of women and their moral superiority and success.

ALAN *is now typing away furiously, trying to keep up with* STEVEN's *narrative.*

ALAN: (*Typing*) You're coming alive, Stevie baby.

STEVEN: Can you get online?

ALAN: Thinks so. Don't know.

STEVEN: You should be able to. Have a quick look at Carvel Collin's structural systems in *The Sound and the Fury* and probably you should have a read on *Ulysses*.

ALAN: *Ulysses*?! I'm not sure I've got time.

STEVEN: Faulkner discovering Joyce.

ALAN: Steve, to be honest, I'm probably cutting it a bit fine. When you say "discovering Joyce", you mean obviously…?

STEVEN: …dispensing with his emulation of Hemingway and Fitzgerald.

ALAN: Right. Of course.

ALAN *begins typing away again.*

STEVEN: If you go with point of view / characterisation, refer to Caddy. He resented the accusations that he was obsessed by the idea that women were the causes of all evil and troubles. He loved Caddy.

ALAN: I'm covering some of this with *The Reivers*. Jesus, you've livened up.

STEVEN: We read to know we're not alone. Fighting isolation. Among shadows. Quentin uses shadows, he lives within shadows. Listen. (*He pulls out a copy of "The Sound and the Fury" from his bag and opens it*). Listen:

> I give (this watch) to you not that you may remember time, but that you might forget it now and then for a moment and not spend all your breath trying to conquer it. Because no battle is ever won he said. They are not even

fought. The field only reveals to man his greatest folly and despair, and victory is an illusion of philosophers and fools.

Silence.

What do you think? A watch so that you might forget time.

ALAN: He is why we do it.

STEVEN: (*Holding up the novel*) Nothing comes close. A painting maybe.

The motor stops. The two men stare out of the window in their own worlds. After some time.

ALAN: What are you going to do, Steve? Steve?

STEVEN: Fuck knows.

ALAN: I mean, is there no way back? I can't believe...

STEVEN: You'll have to talk to her. She doesn't worry. She's set up. Got the house, Jasper, everything. Always the people who've had everything end up with everything. Woman's never had to work in her fucking life. She *has* worked but she didn't have to. It's not the same. Then walks straight in to Finch's. Two years and she brings in three times what I do.

ALAN: It's a different world, mate. It's advertising / media or... what is it – something like that? Different world.

STEVEN: Her dad bought her first flat then ran back to the little corner of the room the fucking

	bitches allow him breath in. He comes out when bills are to be paid.
ALAN:	She's always had a head on her.
STEVEN:	All – who you know.
ALAN:	Fuck, Steve. (*Beat*) Do you want me…? No. I mean I couldn't talk to her…? No. Could I?
STEVEN:	What?
ALAN:	I couldn't talk to her, could I? I mean, I haven't seen her…
STEVE:	Talk to her?
ALAN:	No. Stupid.
STEVEN:	And say what? I just saw Steve on the train and…
ALAN:	No. Daft. Stupid. Just thinking to get her thinking on things. What she's thinking.
STEVEN:	She's thinking – fuck you, I've got a house and kid fuck off.
ALAN:	Sorry, mate. Daft. But you didn't… you haven't done anything…
STEVEN:	I'm… I can be up and down… Alan… to be honest. At times. (*Beat*) Black dog.
ALAN:	Right. Okay.
STEVEN:	Makes me do things. You know. Climbing the muddy pit.
ALAN:	Okay. I've got you. Sorry to hear this, Steve.

Silence. STEVEN looks out the window. Flushed. Sweating. Trying to control his breathing. He turns.

THE DUKE *sits diagonally across from him – nodding. Looking at him. Knowing. He strums his guitar.*

A corona isolates STEVEN. Breathless. Sweating. The corona grows.

STEVEN - ***Running. On a treadmill. A hamster wheel. Desperate. Panting.***

Another corona appears in the distance. Growing larger. SONJA with a child's bag. The corona grows – SONJA in the room. Still STEVEN breathing fast.

JASPER (VOICE ONLY): How long do we have to wait, mummy?

SONJA: Not long, sausage.

JASPER: It's smelly.

SONJA: I know but we won't be long.

JASPER: Where's daddy?

STEVEN – ***Running. Desperate. Panting.***

SONJA: He's running a bit late, babycakes. But he won't be long.

JASPER: I don't like it here.

SONJA: I know. We'll just wait for daddy and then you can go to the park. Daddy'll take you to the park.

JASPER: Why can't daddy come to our house?

SONJA: Because... because he always comes to our house and we thought we'd do something different.

SONJA *sits on the bed looking at* JASPER *who isn't there.*

JASPER: Is this daddy's house now, mummy? Forever?

SONJA: Yes, darling.

JASPER: Why?

SONJA: Because mummy and daddy decided this was the best thing.

JASPER: 'Cos daddy swings?

SONJA: Because of daddy's swings. That's right.

JASPER: I don't think daddy likes his home.

SONJA: But remember that we said that daddy has made his decision. And decisions are important and once you make a decision that's it. Remember?

STEVEN – ***Panting. Gasping.***

JASPER: Yes, I remember. Because of the shouting?

SONJA: That's it, sausage. You didn't like the shouting, did you? Nobody liked the shouting.

JASPER: (*Beat*) Daddy cries sometimes. In the park. He's sad.

SONJA: He is sad, darling. But only for now. He'll be better soon.

Breathing up the stairs. Door handle is rattled and a knock at the door.

STEVEN (V.O): Babe, sorry sorry sorry. Can you let me in?

SONJA *walks over to the door and opens it.* STEVEN *enters – out of breath – holding a carrier bag*

STEVEN: Sorry, I got held up. Everything okay? (*To* JASPER) Hey, Monkey. (*Holding his arms out*) Hey, big monkey.

STEVEN *smothers him in kisses.*

STEVEN: Oh, my little monkey. My little, little monkey. How are you, pardner?

JASPER: Good, daddy.

STEVEN: Missed you so much.

JASPER: Pooh, stinky breath.

STEVEN *looks at* SONJA.

STEVEN: Have I? Sorry, monkey. Daddy'll brush his teeth.

SONJA: You shouldn't leave candles burning.

STEVEN: I know.

SONJA: You'll burn the place down.

STEVEN: I know. I just lit it for a bit. You know, to just…

SONJA: Burn them when you're home not when you're out.

STEVEN: Yes, I know. I was just freshening up the place a bit.

SONJA: His bags on the table. Home by six. Where've you been?

STEVEN:	Sorry, I got caught up.
SONJA:	With what?
STEVEN:	No harm done. Key under the mat and you're in.
SONJA:	If you want him brought round, you have to be here.
STEVEN:	I know. I knew I was going to be pushing it. I left the key. And everything's okay, isn't it.
JASPER:	Can we go to the park now?
STEVEN:	That's exactly where we're going soon as I... (*Opening his plastic bag*) Look what's in here. You'll never guess what daddy got here. He's only got a chuppa chups super cola lolly.
JASPER:	Lolly!
SONJA:	He's already had a treat today.
STEVEN:	Well, he's having another one, isn't he.
SONJA:	Okay, Jasper. You can have the lolly but fruit tomorrow, sausage. Okay? Is that a deal? Fruit tomorrow and another treat on Friday.
STEVEN:	You can have a little treat with daddy.
SONJA:	Yes, you can but fruit tomorrow.
STEVEN:	He can have a treat. It's not a big deal.
SONJA:	I know. He's already had one.
STEVEN:	He can have a treat with me.
SONJA:	Just like his daddy, a treat every day.

STEVEN: Ho ho.

SONJA: Okay, Jasper. Mummy's going. She'll see you in a couple of hours.

JASPER: Noooooo.

STEVEN: It's okay, monkey. We're going to the park. Daddy push you on the swings.

JASPER: Let's go with mummy. Mummy and daddy.

An uneasy moment.

STEVEN: Maybe, mummy would like…

SONJA: Sausage, you're with daddy for a few hours. You can go to the park now and mummy will see you a bit later.

JASPER: Can Jasper, mummy *and* daddy go to the park?

Beat.

SONJA: Do you remember what we talked about, babycakes? Do you remember? About decisions?

JASPER: Yes, mummy.

STEVEN: Decisions?

SONJA: I wouldn't.

STEVEN: Really? Decisions?

SONJA: That's right.

STEVEN: That's all nicely tied up. All boxed and lovely.

SONJA: Okay, sausage. Mummy's going to see you in a couple of hours and she's going to make you a super dazzler dinner.

JASPER: No. Mummy and daddy come to the park. On the swings. Mummy *and* daddy. Please.

SONJA: Jasper, remember what mummy said...?

STEVEN: For fuck's sake, come to the fucking park.

SONJA: Lovely. Fantastic.

STEVEN: Just come to the park. Please. What's the problem? It's the park.

JASPER *holds his hands to his ears. He begins to cry.*

SONJA: Come on, sausage. We're going home.

STEVEN: No, no, no. You're not going home. It's my time. No. For two hours. He's mine. With me. For two fucking hours.

SONJA: Come on, Jasper. Let's go home. Let's get your bag.

SONJA *goes over to the table to pick up* JASPER's *bag.* STEVEN *reaches over, grabs the bag and throws it across the room.*

STEVEN: That bag is going nowhere. And neither is he. For two hours. He's here with me.

SONJA: You don't deserve two minutes. (*Going over to* JASPER) Come on Jasper, let's go home.

STEVEN: (*Going for* SONJA. *Stepping between her and the boy*) I don't think so, honey. No! No, this is my time.

JASPER *cries throughout.*

SONJA: Can you see what you're doing? Look at him. Look what you're doing.

STEVEN: This is my time.

SONJA: Steven, have you seen someone?

STEVEN: Two hours.

SONJA: Steven, have you seen someone again?

STEVEN: That's all.

SONJA: You need to see someone.

STEVEN: All I need. Two hours.

SONJA: You need to call Dr. Mey –

STEVEN: No, no, no, no, no, no!

SONJA: I'm not leaving Jasper here with you in this state –

STEVEN: THIS IS MY TIME! THIS IS MY TIME. THEY SAID, IT WAS MY TIME!!!!

SONJA: (*Breaking*) YOU'VE HAD YOUR TIME! Most of your life was your time. And you want more. I gave you two hours. I gave them to you. What an idiot. Two hours of your... Steven, I have to go. I can't do this. Look at him. I can't have you filling him with this bile. Sorry.

STEVEN: HE'S NOT YOURS. HE'S OURS. HE'S NOT YOUR PROPERTY. HE'S OURS. BOTH OF US. HE'S *OURS*.

SONJA: I CAN'T TAKE ANYMORE!!!! STEVEN. FUCK. PLEASE. I CAN'T.

JASPER *is wailing.*

SONJA: Listen to him. (*To* JASPER) Ok darling, we're going. (*Back to*) Steven, you're poisoning him with all this. You're poisoning everyone. I can't do this. You stink of booze and... it's just... I can't do it.

STEVEN: You've ruined this family and you can't even see it. You come from a family of female obsessives. Ask your mother. An army of fucking tortuous ball breakers. The lot of you, you, your sisters, your mother, the whole fucking lot, smothering him your web. He's fucking choking.

SONJA: You're sick. Really, Steven. You're ill. And you need to call Dr. Meyers. I can't. That's it. You need to get... I don't know. Jasper can't be here. Ever (*To* JASPER) Come on, sausage. Let's go.

STEVEN: Go. Go on fucking go. FUCKING GO.

SONJA *exits with* JASPER. STEVEN *slams the door after them. He then re-opens it and screams down the stairs.*

STEVEN: FUCKING GO CUNT BITCH.

He slams the door. He stands motionless in the room. FUCKING GO CUNT BITCH bounces off the walls repeatedly within the echo chamber. Darkness descends.

STEVEN - *fights the darkness. Punching. Kicking out against it. Exhausted – puts his hands to his head. His head is a pressure cooker that suddenly shoots whistling steam out of the top. Out of the darkness.*

STEVEN - *head is in a bottle like a preserved specimen.*

He looks round. ALAN *is typing into his laptop.*

ALAN: We should have a drink, you know. On the way back. Do you want to? What train you getting back?

STEVEN: I'm not.

ALAN: You're not coming back?

STEVEN: No.

ALAN: You got family up here? You're from up here, aren't you?

STEVEN: Macclesfield. Originally. My mum and dad are still there.

ALAN: Right. So, you gonna see them?

STEVEN: Maybe. Not sure.

ALAN: Right.

The train begins to slow down. Stoke on Trent station comes into view.

ALAN: Fuck. Here we go. It's Hopalong Cassidy again.

STEVEN: Who?

ALAN: That Duke bloke's coming.

THE DUKE *appears at the table.*

THE DUKE: Their snouts failed to locate the Duke.

STEVEN: How long were you in the toilet?

THE DUKE: What is time, amigo. I came and went. Not nappies, old phones, hopes, dreams, goldfish, ex-sweaters or flange towels down the bowl.

ALAN: On the seats.

THE DUKE: Tippa-tappy tippa-tappy, tippa-tappy, tippa-tappy – those silver boxes. (*On* ALAN's *laptop*) Boxes of nothing. To do nothing.

ALAN: It's a bit more complex than that...

THE DUKE: Sure it is.

THE DUKE *sniffs the air and looks at* STEVEN

THE DUKE: Yes, yes, yes. Some seek the singer of sad songs.

STEVEN: To sing.

THE DUKE *strums his guitar and sings gently. He sings the chorus of "SINGER OF SAD SONGS" by Waylon Jennings*

STEVEN: Yes.

THE DUKE: Some seek.

STEVEN – *A knock.*

THE DUKE: To sympathise and eulogise.

STEVEN: Yes...to...

STEVEN – ***Knock knock.***

STEVEN *is stood by the door inside his bedsit – his jacket over his shoulder and bag on the floor. Listening.* FOLAMI *is on the other side of the door.*

FOLAMI: (*Knocking*) Steven?

STEVEN *listens at the door.*

FOLAMI: Steven? Are you in there?

STEVEN *motionless – ear to the door.*

FOLAMI: (*Calling*) Steven? Steven? (*Beat*) Steven, I have someone coming for you. Steven?! It is Folami – from before. Remember? Open the door please, Steven. Steven? I have someone who can help you. Talk to you and help. (*Listening at the door – her face almost touching* STEVEN's *between the door*) Are you in there, Steven? It is Folami – I said I would come back – remember? Open the door, Steven. I have someone coming – a colleague – who can talk to you. Are you in there?

STEVEN *still motionless.*

FOLAMI *backs away from the door. She turns to go – a last look – and walks away. Footsteps.*

STEVEN *turns his head to the door.* **She's gone now.**

STEVEN: Where are you going... Duke?

THE DUKE: Where do we go?

ALAN: No, where are you going when we get to –

THE DUKE: – the final destination? The end –

STEVEN: – of the line.

STEVEN - ***The flapping of wings in his ears. Around his head. Rattling – then clicking and a kraa. Flapping.***

THE DUKE: It's the wind.

STEVEN: Are you staying?

THE DUKE: For winter.

ALAN: What are you doing up in Manchester? What's your business?

THE DUKE: No business.

STEVEN – ***Footsteps – young, running. A child's laughter.***

He picks JASPER *up in his arms. Hugs him into himself until the boy disappears into him.*

STEVEN: Have you got children, Duke?

THE DUKE: Maybe. The seed is strong.

ALAN: One's you know of?

THE DUKE: What is knowing. With a woman. Only they know.

ALAN: You know what I mean.

THE DUKE: When the bitches give off their scent the sires circle.

ALAN: Right. So take your pick, that's you?

THE DUKE: Man looks, desires. Convict a man for what he thinks – the streets will be empty and the prisons full.

ALAN: So, what your saying is…? What are you saying? Fuck it, women come, women go? Is that it? Just a-copulating. Dust yourself off and move on.

THE DUKE: These are the words of the liar in the woods. The liar of the woods convinces himself that he is master of everything. But, the reality is the bear is the master.

ALAN *laughs.*

ALAN: Sorry, look fascinating as it is, we're not too sure what your acquaintance with reality is. Exactly.

Awkward silence.

I mean, generally speaking. You know what I mean? I know it's all a bit of fun. Bit of banter. A good old yarn approach thing.

THE DUKE: I take your meaning, compadre.

ALAN: Sorry, you know what I mean. You've got a way with words. Tell a good old tale. It's entertaining.

THE DUKE: I understand. (*Taking his guitar out of it case*) Speak your mind.

THE DUKE *begins strumming his guitar gently.*

ALAN: Nothing in it. Either way. What we're discussing. Trying to find... is answers. No, solutions. To this problem. This situation. Of Steve's. That's it.

THE DUKE: (*Strumming*) I see. I see. Yes. Solutions. Solutions to problems... in this world. I see.

THE DUKE *begins to sing "WAITING AROUND TO DIE" by Townes Van Zandt (Verses 1, 2 and 4)*

STEVEN – *Mesmerised – trance-like. Again wings flapping. Deeper. Dark wings swirl around him.*

STEVEN: Kill the pain.

ALAN: That was good. Lovely tune. Who is that?

THE DUKE: A song from along the way.

ALAN: Is it yours?

THE DUKE: The songs I sing are all mine.

STEVEN: What happens when the train stops?

THE DUKE: We are at an end.

ALAN: To you? He means to you. Don't you, Steve?

THE DUKE: To me?

ALAN: What are you doing when you get there? Isn't it, Steve?

STEVEN: At the end. Where do you go?

THE DUKE: What is on the horizon? Look into it.

STEVEN: Yes.

STEVEN *motionless. Silence. But floating now out of himself.* ALAN *becomes a fluid distant mass – shimmering.* THE DUKE *is a diamond.*

THE DUKE: Can you see it?

STEVEN: The...?

ALAN: Steve?

THE DUKE: The snake.

ALAN: Steve?

STEVEN: Yes.

THE DUKE: Sheds it's skin.

STEVEN: And begins again.

THE DUKE:	Yes. But with venom.
ALAN:	Steve?
THE DUKE:	Move along.
ALAN:	What?
THE DUKE:	You heard.
STEVEN:	To...?
THE DUKE:	Be sure the mountain moon doesn't set on you. The snake finds everyone.
ALAN:	What are you...?!
THE DUKE:	His eyes are diamonds.
STEVEN:	He sees you come back...
ALAN:	Steve!!!???
THE DUKE:	Yes, a return. Can be.
ALAN:	What?!
THE DUKE:	But more – sanctuary.

STEVEN – *Begins to choke. Coughs out dust. Choking and coughing. The carriage begins to fill with dust. Looks up at* THE DUKE *who is now a raven. Perched on the headrest opposite. He kraas and flaps his wings.*

And then ALAN *is standing over* STEVEN *loosening his shirt, leaning him forward as he coughs and chokes.*

ALAN: Steve!!! Jesus! Steve!! All right, mate! Steve!!! Breathe. Breathe, mate. Breathe. Deep breaths. (*Breathing with him*) In, out. In, out.

And locusts now – through the dust – hitting STEVEN. *Coughing in the dust – brushing them away.*

ALAN: Keep breathing. In and out. That's it.

STEVEN: Water.

ALAN: Water? Do you want water?

STEVEN: Water.

ALAN: Jesus, Steve! What... I mean... Are you taking anything?

Piercing white noise. Feedback. Through it – blue light siren. Rush of the train in a tunnel – amplifying – heightening the rush.

STEVEN: Water.

ALAN: Seriously, Steve. Are you on anything? You know, to help. Keep breathing. In and out.

STEVEN: Just need some water.

ALAN: Water. Right. Do you need to take anything?

STEVEN: For my mouth. Some just water.

ALAN: Okay. Water – (*reaching for his bag*) I've got some. Here (*Handing him the bottle of water*) Steve?

STEVEN – *Drinks. Coughs. Takes out a small mirror from his pocket – raises it – looks up into it to look at the top of his head. An opening – a door - to reach in*

STEVEN: Can you get in?

ALAN: What? Where?

STEVEN: (*Hand to head*) Can you get in here? Take it out.

ALAN: I don't...

STEVEN: Take it out. Pull it out and take out that bit. Pull the whole thing out!

ALAN: Steve... I don't know... take what out!?

STEVEN: The bad... take out that.

ALAN: Steve... I don't know what...?

STEVEN: (*Pointing into his head – looking into mirror*) Here! Here! Take it out!

ALAN: What?! What, Steve?

STEVEN: Can you see it?

ALAN: Have some more water, Steve.

NEARING (THEN ME, NOW ME)

TANNOY: (*Distorted, muffled, echoed*) We will shortly be arriving at Manchester Piccadilly. We'd like to take this opportunity to thank you for travelling on Virgin trains. And hope you have a safe onward journey.

ALAN: Steve, drink. Look, what do you want to do?

STEVEN *looks at him.*

ALAN: Are you going to make this?

FOLAMI: Open the door, Steven.

ALAN: We need to cancel today, Steve. Keep breathing.

STEVEN: Fine.

ALAN: Could tell them you took ill on the journey.

STEVEN: I'm fine.

ALAN: Steve...

THE DUKE: Think he said he's fine. Or am I cloth ears?

THE DUKE *is there. The train surges – jolts – begins to speed up.*

ALAN: You don't have to, Steve.

STEVEN: I'm going.

THE DUKE: Sure you are.

STEVEN: Yes.

THE DUKE: All the way.

The train accelerates.

ALAN: You need to rest, Steve. Take it easy –

THE DUKE: It's so easy.

SONJA: What did I just say?

STEVEN: We should invite them.

SONJA: What do you think?

STEVEN: Yes, invite them.

ALAN: I could talk to them, Steve. Say you're not –

THE DUKE: So easy.

The train is hurtling now. ALAN *begins to clutch the headrest of the seat to steady himself.*

STEVEN: I could just pick him up early on Thursdays.

SONJA: Could you?

STEVEN: I could. We'll pull him out. I'll pick him up on Thursdays.

SONJA: Can you? I wouldn't get here in time.

STEVEN: I'll do it.

STEVEN: We read to know we're not alone. Among shadows. Quentin uses shadows, he lives within shadows... Because no battle is ever won he said... victory is an illusion of philosophers and fools.

The carriage is a wind tunnel now and ALAN *is horizontal – hanging on to the headrest.* STEVEN *is seated in silent scream.* THE DUKE *watches above and beyond in his form.*

STEVEN: What happens when the train stops?

THE DUKE: We are at an end.

ALAN: To you? He means to you. Don't you, Steve?

THE DUKE: To me?

ALAN: Isn't it, Steve?

STEVEN: At the end. Where do you go?

JASPER: Can we go to the park now?

STEVEN: That's exactly where we're going.

STEVEN: You said... you were staying.

FOLAMI: I'm going to get you help.

STEVEN: No. You said...

FOLAMI: I can get someone who can help.

STEVEN: You said... you were... you were...

ALAN *is struggling to hold on to the headrest. The train is hurtling, wind rushing. A crescendo.*

SONJA: You've had your time.

ALAN: I could talk to them.

FOLAMI: I can get someone who can help.

STEVEN: Does it end?

JASPER: Can Jasper, mummy *and* daddy go to the park?

THE DUKE: Yes.

ALAN: Steve?!

STEVEN: The pain?

THE DUKE: Yes. Solace is there.

SONJA: You want to infect that child?!

JASPER: Mummy *and* Daddy.

STEVEN: Solace.

FOLAMI: I will bring someone.

SONJA: You were born lying.

THE DUKE: No more troubles.

STEVEN *looks up bedlinen in his hand. Begins to stand. Wind rushing in his head.*

ALAN: What are you going to do, Steve?

STEVEN: I've just got to...

SONJA: What did you have for lunch?

JASPER: (*Singing/nursery rhyme*) The wheels of the train go round and round, round and round. (*Repeat rhyme*).

THE DUKE: Some seek the singer of sad songs.

ALAN: It's the distance between us.

SONJA: Not all of a sudden a family man?

ALAN: The optimum distance.

STEVEN: I just...

THE DUKE: The time has come.

SONJA: You have to ruin everything.

THE DUKE: Seal the river at its mouth. We'll tell the world we tried.

Rushing rushing rushing sound. The screeching sound of breaks, metal wheels scrape metal tracks. A howling whistle. Screams. Then black silence.

STEVEN – **hands to head. Silent scream – inside. Winter in the mind – wailing – within. Bacon's middle triptych. Whirligig. Chaos. Silent. Confines of a room.**

Puts his hands out calmly in front of him and makes two fists. His body becomes a fist. Focused. In ritual. Silent – voiceless muttering. Reaches down with studied precision to a bottle of brandy. Bottle to mouth. Mechanical. Takes one shot. Exact. He lifts his hands to the ceiling. Reaches down. Finds it. Looks up. STEVEN *raises himself from the chair... ...*

END